LOLA RACE CARS
1962 - 1990
Photo Album

Text and Photographs by
Norman Hayes

Iconografix

Photo Album Series

Iconografix continuously seeks collections of archival photographs for reproduction in future books. We require a minimum of 120 photographs per subject. We prefer subjects narrow in focus, i.e., a specific model, railroad, racing venue, etc. Photographs must be of high-quality, suited to reproduction in an 8x10-inch format. We willingly pay for the use of photographs.

If you own or know of such a collection, please contact: The Publisher, Iconografix, PO Box 446, Hudson, Wisconsin 54016.

Iconografix
PO Box 446
Hudson, Wisconsin 54016 USA

Text Copyright © 1997

Iconografix books are offered at a discount when sold in quantity for promotional use. Businesses or organizations seeking details should write to the Marketing Department, Iconografix, at the above address.

Library of Congress Card Number 97-70641

ISBN 1-882256-73-5

97 98 99 00 01 02 03 5 4 3 2 1

Printed in the United States of America

Mike Hailwood, in his Lola T142, competing in the 1969 Guards 5000 Guineas Race at Oulton Park, the first Formula 5000 race run in England. The T142 was powered by a 5.0-liter Traco-Chevrolet V-8.

INTRODUCTION

Eric Broadley began his racing career in 1955, sharing a 750-cc special owned by his cousin. In 1956, he built an 1172-cc special called a "Lola". Broadley raced the car during the 1957 season with some success. He decided to commit himself to professional racing, but came up against serious opposition. Although Broadley had been successful in club racing, it was a different situation when competing against the likes of Graham Hill and John Surtees. Being completely out of his depth, Broadley gave up racing and concentrated on building cars.

Broadley had no training as an automotive engineer. He had worked in the building trade as a surveyor, which had included some drawing board experience that proved valuable in designing cars. Broadley built three cars for the 1958/59 season. Designated MK Is, they were equipped with Coventry Climax engines. Lotus driver Peter Ashdown was invited to try out the car over the winter period, and he opened Broadley's eyes at the speeds that he could achieve in his car. The first race for the three cars was at the prestigious Goodwood Easter Monday Sports Car event. The cars occupied the first three places on the grid. From the start they had a private race between themselves, drawing rapidly away from the rest of the field, and finishing 1-2-3 by a large margin. Throughout the season, the car was the most successful in its class, both in Britain and abroad. People were queuing up to purchase Lola cars, which Broadley was building on a full-time basis in a small shop outside London. In all, there were 36 MK 1 cars built. In 1960, he produced a front-engined Formula Junior car, designated the MK 2. Although the MK 2 was not as successful as the MK 1, Lola cars dominated the Formula Junior races that year.

For the 1962 season, Broadley was commissioned to build a Formula 1 car by Bowmaker-Yeoman, a finance company which had sponsored John Surtees during the 1961 season. The team was run by the ex-driver Reg Parnell. Designated the MK 4, the car was of conventional design. It was initially powered by a 4-cylinder Coventry-Climax engine, but was soon replaced with a V-8 from the same company. The car was driven quite successfully by Surtees in many non-championship races during the year. His best finish was a third place in the International Trophy Race at Silverstone. Surtees and his teammate Roy Salvadori debuted the

MK 4 in the world championship races at Zandvoort. Surtees won the pole position, but during the race retired when the suspension broke. Second place in both the British and German Grand Prix were the best results of the season for the MK 4. Parnell ran the cars again during the 1963 season. His drivers, the young New Zealander Chris Amon, World Motor Cycle champion Mike Hailwood, and French Grand Prix winner Maurice Trintignant, did not have much success, as the cars were becoming outclassed. Consequently, Lola moved away from Grand Prix cars to concentrate on sports cars and other smaller classes of racing cars.

One of the next cars produced by Lola was the GT6, a beautiful looking sports car with Ford 4.2-liter V-8 and a central monocoque. The GT6 was eventually developed by Ford Motor Company (with help from Broadley, among others) into the GT40. Once Broadley had finished his work on the Ford GT project, he concentrated on building a new Lola sports car, the T70.

The first Lola T70s were built in 1965. It was a very fast car. Surtees set up what was effectively a works race team, and their early trials with the car produced record-breaking top speeds. A range of V-8 engines was used in the cars: first, a 4.5-liter Traco Oldsmobile; then, a 4.5-liter Chevrolet; later in the year a 5.9-liter Traco Chevrolet. A Ford 4.7-liter V-8 was also used, but it proved too slow to compete with the 5.9-liter Chevy cars. Halfway through the 1965 season, Broadley redesigned the T70, cutting its weight and designating it the T70 MK II. The T70 became a consistent winner in the sports car class and, in particular, in Can-Am racing. Surtees became the first Can-Am champion in 1966, driving the T70. The title was won a further five times by the Lola cars. For 1967, Lola developed the MK II into the MK III. Both open and coupe bodies were offered, and the cars were still fitted with the Chevrolet V-8. 1969 saw an all new coupe, designated the MK IIIB, of which there were only 16 built. The Lola T70 was very popular with privateers, who won many non-championship races. Yet, in all the time that the Lola T70 was raced, it won only one World Sports Car Championship event—Daytona in 1969.

Broadley exploited the Indianapolis race and produced the T90 for Graham Hill, who drove it took first at the 500-mile event in 1966.

Lola has since produced many cars for CART teams, with Nigel Mansell winning the championship in one of the cars in 1993.

About the time that the T70 became obsolete, in the late 1960s, Formula 5000 racing was beginning in Britain. The first race of the series was held at Oulton Park on Good Friday 1969. The Lola T142, equipped with a 5-liter Chevrolet V-8, became one of the most successful F5000 racing cars. The T142 was succeeded by the T190 in 1970. The T190 suffered from handling problems, which were cured by lengthening the car's wheelbase. This was first done by privateer Frank Gardner, with other Lola car owners following suit. After the successful modifications to his own car, Gardner was enrolled on the development staff of Lola Cars. He continued driving and went on to win the Rothmans F5000 Championship in the T190 and its successor the T300. (The Lola T330 followed in 1972; the T332 in 1974. F5000 faded out in mid-1970s, and no more of the big-engined cars were built.)

Graham Hill, ex-Formula 1 World Champion, set up his own Formula 1 team in 1973 using a Shadow car. Disappointed with its performance, he asked Broadley to build a new car for 1974. Designated the T370, it evolved as the T371. Redesigned by a former Lola employee for the 1975 season, the car emerged as the Hill GH1. (After Hill retired from racing, GH1 was driven with more success by the up-and-coming young Tony Brise. Hill, Brise, and other Hill team members were killed in an air crash in 1976.)

In 1978, Al Unser, driving a Lola T500, became the first driver ever to win all three American 500-mile races in one season, finishing in second place in the Indy Car Championship. During the 1978 season, Indy cars raced in England at both Silverstone and Brands Hatch, as part of the championship series. This was the start of Lola competing regularly in Indy Car racing. In 1983, Mario Andretti, driving a Lola T700, finished 3rd overall in the championship; in 1984, he won the series again with a Lola T800. Both of Andretti's cars were powered by a Ford-Cosworth engine. Lola's Indy Car racing wins continued: in 1987, Bobby Rahal (T87/00); 1990 (the last year covered by this book), Al Unser, Jr., (T90/01); 1991, Michael Andretti (T91/00); 1992, Bobby Rahal ((T92/00); and 1993 Nigel Mansell (T93/00).

Lola returned to Formula 1 racing in 1985. Carl Hass, the US importer of Lola, and Teddy Mayer set up the FORCE (Formula One Race Car Engineering) Formula 1 operation. Major sponsorship came from the American food company Beatrice. Their car was the THL-1, and former World Champion Alan Jones was employed to drive it. The season did not start well for the team. A new Ford-Cosworth engine planned for the car was not ready to race, and a 1.5-liter Hart 4-cylinder turbo engine was used instead. Because of the delay, the team competed in only the final four races of the year, starting with the Italian G.P. at Monza. It was quite an unrewarding four races, with a retirement in each. Patrick Tambay was signed as the second driver for the 1986 season. The Ford engine was still not race worthy, and for the first two races they ran with the Hart engine. The cars had been updated and were numbered THL-2. The Ford engine, a 1.5 V-6 turbo, ran its first race in Jones' car at the San Marino G.P., but retired when it overheated. During the season, Jones was only in the points on two occasions, with a 4th in the Austrian G.P. and a 6th at Monza in the Italian G.P. Tambay fared no better, with only a 5th in the Austrian G.P. Eddie Cheever raced the car in the US G.P. but, like the other drivers, had no success. Cheever retired with no drive to the wheels. The team folded at the end of 1986.

Lola was still around in 1987, however. Gerard Larrousse, a former driver and employee of Renault, started his own team, using Eric Broadley's Lola cars for five seasons. The Larrousse team used a number of drivers during this period: Yannick Dalmas and Phillipe Alliot for the first three years, who, between them, scored only five championship points; Eric Bernard and Aguri Suzuki in 1990 and 1991. Bernard and Suzuki were a little more successful than Dalmas and Alliot. Bernard placed 4th in one race and scored three 6th place finishes; Suzuki placed 3rd in the 1990 Japanese G.P. (Suzuki was only the second driver to achieve a podium position in a Lola F1 car, the other being John Surtees). During the five seasons, the Larrousse Lola's used a variety of engines: for the first two years, the Ford-Cosworth DFZ V-8; in 1989 and 1990, a Lamborghini V-12; in 1991, the Ford-Cosworth DER V-8 and the Hart V-8.

I have had the opportunity to witness and photograph Lola cars for nearly 30 years, beginning with Broadley's first Formula 1 car. The cars in *Lola Race Cars 1965-1990 Photo Album* were photographed at various venues in England. Included are an exciting variety of cars—true testimony to the genius of Eric Broadley and to the longevity and success of Lola Cars.

Norman Hayes
November 1996

John Surtees and Masten Gregory (back to camera) stand by Surtee's MK 4-Climax V-8 (T4-V8) in the Oulton Park paddock prior to the 1962 Gold Cup race. A keen supporter of Eric Broadley, Surtees was a significant figure in Lola's early years. He drove the first Lola Formula 1 cars, and later won the first Can-Am championship driving the legendary Lola T70.

The MK 4-Climax 4 (4-cylinder T4) of Roy Salvadori at Aintree for the 1962 International 200 Race. Salvadori's car was retired in lap eight with a broken throttle. Surtees ran well with a MK 4-Climax V-8 (T4-V8), until engine problems forced his retirement.

A very young Chris Amon leaving the paddock at the 1963 International 200 Race. The 19-year old New Zealander drove his T4-V8 to a sixth-place finish.

Mike Hailwood, then reigning World Motor Cycle Champion, in his T4-V8 during the 1963 Oulton Park Gold Cup race. Hailwood drove the Lola to a seventh-place finish.

The Formula 2 Lola-Climax of Paul Hawkins in the paddock at Oulton Park for the 1964 Gold Cup.

Hawkins' F2 Lola-Climax took fifth place in the 1964 Gold Cup race.

John Surtees with his mechanic in the paddock at Oulton Park prior to the 1965 Tourist Trophy race. This early Type 70 (T70) was fitted with a 5.9-liter Chevrolet engine modified by Traco.

Surtees on the track at Oulton Park for the 1965 Tourist Trophy race. His T70 developed problems and did not finish the race.

Surtees in his 998-cc Lola-Cosworth, prior to the Oulton Park 1965 International Gold Cup for Formula 2 cars. Surtees started from ninth place on the grid but went on to win.

Denny Hulme's T70 in the paddock at Oulton Park prior to the 1966 Tourist Trophy race. Hulme won the 31st Tourist Trophy race by five laps.

The 1966 Tourist Trophy race also featured this unusual T70, on which were fixed cine' cameras back and front. Warner Bros. were using the race for their film *Day of the Champion*.

Phil Scragg in his 4.7-liter Lola T70 Ford Special at the start of a run of the 1967 Barbon Manor hill climb.

Scragg set Best Time of the Day and established a new hill record at Barbon Manor.

The Lola T70 of C. Darlington during the 1967 Oulton Park Tourist Trophy race.

The T70 MK 3 of Brian Redman used a 5.0-liter Chevrolet engine to power him to a crushing victory at the 1968 Guards Spring Cup race at Oulton Park.

Hulme in his 5-liter Lola-Chevrolet T70 MK 3 GT led a Porsche at Knickerbrook Corner during the 1968 R.A.C. Tourist Trophy race at Oulton Park.

Jo Bonnier's MK 3 GT was forced from second place into retirement, when a fuel tank split at the 1968 R.A.C. Tourist Trophy race.

The combination of Hulme and Lola proved unbeatable, with Hulme winning the 33rd R.A.C. Tourist Trophy in 1968.

Denny Hulme in the paddock after winning the 1968 R.A.C. Tourist Trophy event.

Jo Bonnier led the field away from the start of the 1968 Sports Car Race at Oulton Park in his 5.0-liter T70 MK 3 GT.

Mike de Udy's 5.0-liter T70-Chevrolet during the 1968 Oulton Park Sports Car Race.

Bonnier held the lead throughout the 1968 Oulton Park Sports Car Race, until...

... his collision with another competitor. Bonnier spun off the track and lost half a minute recovering. He lost first place but finished second.

Mike Walker's Lola-Bartz-Chevrolet T142 (above and right) suffered serious overheating problems during the 1969 Guards 5000 Race at Oulton Park. Walker kept the car going to take the flag in seventh place.

William Forbes' Lola Tl42 with Traco-Chevrolet V-8, during the 1969 Guards 5000 Race. Forbes spun out of the race at Knickerbrook Corner.

Ulf Norinder in his Lola T142 during the 1969 Guards 5000 Race. Norinder finished in fifth place.

Hailwood's Lola-Traco-Chevrolet T142 during the 1969 Guards 5000 Race. Hailwood ran for most of the race in third place, but a driveshaft broke and mutilated the suspension causing his retirement.

Mike Hailwood in the paddock at Oulton Park prior to the 1969 Guards 5000 Race.

Hailwood (no. 21) and Peter Gethin in a McLaren M10A approaching Lodge Corner during the 1969 Guards 5000 race.

Horst Kroll driving a T142 at Knickerbrook Corner, during the 1969 Guards 5000 race. Kroll finished the race in sixth place.

Norinder leads Doug Hardwick at Knickerbrook Corner during the 1969 Guards 5000 Race.

Hardwick drove his Lola T142 to fourth place at the 1969 Guards 5000 Race.

David Hobbs (no. 15) in a Surtees TS5 leads Hailwood at Knickerbrook Corner during the 1969 Guards 5000 race.

Car no. 1, the Paul Hawkins/Jonathan Williams 5.0-liter T70 MK 3-Chevrolet, neck-and-neck with the David Piper/Pierpoint 5.0-liter T70 MK 3-Chevrolet, at Pilgrims Drop Brands Hatch for the 1969 BOAC International 500-mile Sports Car race.

The Ulf Norinder/Robin Widdows T70 MK 3B suffered a broken rear wishbone during the 1969 BOAC 500 Sports Car race. It was repaired, and the pair finished in 21st place.

The winning car at the 1969 BOAC 500 Sports Car race, Siffert and Redman's Porsche 908, passes the Lola T70 of Taylor and Dibley.

The 34th Tourist Trophy at Oulton Park in 1969 went to Trevor Taylor, driving a Lola-Chevrolet T70 MK 3B (car no. 36) to his first major victory since leaving Lotus in 1962.

Trevor Taylor's T70 throws up the spray during a rainy period of the 1969 Tourist Trophy race.

Paul Hawkins in his T70 MK 3B during the 1969 Tourist Trophy race. Hawkins put a wheel onto the grass on lap 75, spun out of control, hitting a marshal's post and then a tree. The car exploded in flames, and Hawkins was killed.

Paul Hawkins in the paddock at Oulton Park prior to the 1969 Tourist Trophy.

David Piper took second in the 1969 Tourist Trophy in his T70 MK 3B.

Brian Redman punctured a tire of his T70 MK 3 on lap 35 while leading, spun into a bank, and later retired from the 34th Tourist Trophy race.

Mac Daghorn in a Ford GT40 leads Piper's T70 MK 3 at Old Hall Corner during the 1969 Tourist Trophy race.

Jo Bonnier (right) and Graham Hill in conversation outside the scrutineering bay, before the 1969 International Gold Cup race at Oulton Park. Bonnier drove a Lotus 49 for the combined F1 and F5000 event, and qualified a T70 for the sports car support race. He crashed the Lotus and was unable to race his Lola.

Bonnier's T70 MK 3B-Chevrolet V-8 qualified in the pole position for the 1969 Gold
Cup sports car race.

Frank Gardner (right) and Jack Brabham discuss the relative merits of Gardner's Lola T70 prior to the 1969 International Gold Cup event.

The T70 MK 2B-Chevrolet of Gardner at Lodge Corner during the support race for the 1969 Gold Cup. Gardner won the sports car race with relative ease.

Mike Hailwood studies his enormous-looking F5000 Lola T142 Chevrolet-engined car in the paddock before the 1969 Gold Cup race.

Hailwood's Lola T142 on its way to a fifth-place finish in the combined F1 and F5000 race for the 1969 International Gold Cup.

Derrick Williams' Lola-Chevrolet T142 during the 1969 Guards 5000 race. Williams finished in fifth place.

Winner of the 1969 Guards Oulton 5000 race, Mike Walker (above and right), in his Lola-Chevrolet T142.

Mike Hailwood secured the pole position for the 1969 Guards 5000 race in his Lola-Chevrolet T142. During the race, Hailwood spun off the track and into retirement.

Norinder took fourth place in the 1969 Guards 5000 race in his T142-Chevrolet.

William Forbes' T142 led Williams' T142 through Old Hall Corner during the 1969 Guards 5000 race.

The Jo Bonnier and Reine Wisell 5-liter T70 MK 3B GT-Chevrolet finished the 1970 BOAC 1000 Kilometer race at Brands Hatch in seventh place—the only Lola to finish the race.

The Bonnier/Wisell T70 leads the Porsche 917 of Hermann and Attwood during the 1970 BOAC 1000 race.

Willie Forbes' T142 with 5-liter Traco-Chevrolet V-8, in the paddock prior to the 1970 BRSCC race at Oulton Park. Forbes drove a sensible, controlled race to take fourth, the best finish of the day for Lola.

The Traco-Chevrolet engine in Forbes' Lola T142.

Brazilian Carlos Avallone in his Lola T140-Traco Chevrolet for the 1970 BRSCC race. Avallone suffered superficial burns to the legs, when his car burst into flames following an accident on the first lap.

Mike Hailwood in the assembly area prior to the BRSCC 5000 race at Oulton Park in 1970. Hailwood was leading the race when he spun his T190 into retirement.

Ian Ashley crashed his T142 during practice, damaging the chassis and keeping him out of the race. His boss, Ulf Norinder, drove his T190 to a ninth-place finish.

Frank Gardner drove his 5-liter T300-Smith-Chevrolet to first place at the 1971 Rothmans International Gold Cup at Oulton Park.

Frank Gardner in the paddock area of Oulton Park during the Rothmans International Gold Cup in 1971. Gardner, whose successful modifications to his own Lola T190 had recently earned him a spot on Lola's development staff, was the 1971 Rothman F5000 Champion.

Mike Walker finished sixth in the 1971 Gold Cup F5000 race in his T190-Smith-Chevrolet.

No. 12, Alan Rollinson, leads the field at the start of the F5000 race at the 1972 Gold Cup race at Oulton Park.

Rollinson's T300-Smith-Chevrolet retired from the 1972 Gold Cup meeting with a broken rear cross member.

Gardner in a Lola T330-Chevrolet at Druids Corner Brands Hatch for the 1972 John Players Victory meeting. He was driving a brand new car, and was quite happy to finish the race in third place.

Guy Edwards' T330 went off the track during the warm-up session for the Rothmans 5000 race at Oulton Park in 1973. The front end was damaged beyond immediate repair.

Guy Edwards walks back to his pits after
damaging his Lola beyond repair at the 1973
Rothmans 5000 race.

David Hobbs' 5.0-liter Lola-Morand-Chevrolet T330. The engine let go in a great cloud of white smoke on lap 24 of the 1973 GKN Daily Express Silver Jubilee Trophy at Silverstone.

Graham Hill driving a T370 with 3-liter Cosworth-Ford DFV V-8 for the 1974 International Trophy. Hill retired on lap 31 with a broken suspension. Commissioned by Hill for his Embassy Racing Formula 1 team, the Lola T370 was replaced by the T371 (developed by a former Lola employee), which was renamed the Hill GH1.

Richard Scott's Formula Atlantic 1.6-liter Lola-Ford at a support race for the 1974 International Trophy race.

Bob Evans' Lola-Smith-Chevrolet T332 lead for most of the race for the 1974 Gold Cup. A tire suffered a puncture, which dropped Evans back to sixth place.

Ian Ashley was winner of the 1974 Gold Cup at Oulton Park in his Lola T330.

Ashley drives down Deers Leap on his way to winning the 1974 Gold Cup at Oulton Park.

Keith Holland, in his T332-Smith-Chevrolet, finished third in the 1974 Gold Cup race at Oulton Park.

Nick Wattiez finished 10th in the 1974 Oulton Park Gold Cup race in his Lola T330.

Lella Lombardi finished fourth in the 1974 Oulton Park Gold Cup race in this Lola T330 with 5-liter Fawkes-Chevrolet V-8.

Martin Raymond's 2-liter Lola-Ford T390 finished fifth in the 2-liter Sports Car race at Silverstone in 1975.

Guy Edwards took second in the 2-liter Sports Car race at Silverstone in 1975 in his Ford-powered Lola T390.

Nigel Clarkson's 2-liter T294-Ford FVC at Woodcote Corner during the Group 5 Sports Car race at Silverstone in 1975. Clarkson finished in 10th place.

Ted Wentz finished sixth in the Formula Atlantic race at Silverstone in 1975 in his 1.6-liter T360-Ford BDA.

Hill in the 3-liter Hill-Ford-Cosworth DFV V-8 car. Designated a "Hill" car, it was based on the Lola T370. Hill finished in 11th place for the 1975 Silverstone BRDC International Trophy.

Car no. 7, Derek Daly's T490, leads the field at Knickerbrook Corner during the 1977 Sports Car race at Oulton Park. Daily came home in first place.

Al Unser in his Lola-Ford-Cosworth T500 during the 1978 Daily Express Indy car race at Silverstone, round 16 of the USAC Championship.

Unser at Woodcote during the 1978 Indy race at Silverstone. He failed to finish when the Lola's crown wheel and pinion broke on the 26th lap.

John Brindley finished fourth in the 1978 Sports Car race at Silverstone in a 2-liter Ford-powered Lola 492.

Alo Lawler's T460-Smith-Ford finished seventh in the Formula Atlantic race at Oulton Park 1979.

Car no. 51, Mike Blanchet's Chevrolet-powered Lola 672, at Oulton Park during a Formula 3 race in 1979.

Emilo de Villota and Guy Edwards' T600-Ford led the 1981 World Sports Car Race at Silverstone until half distance, when it ran out of fuel.

The Guy Edwards and Rupert Keegan 3-liter T610-Ford-Cosworth had many problems during the 1982 World Sports Car Race at Silverstone causing them long delays.

Edwards and Keegan finished the 1982 World Sports Car Race in 16th place.

Gerry Marshall's 5-liter Lola-Chevrolet T222, the ex-Chuck Parson's Can-Am chassis, at a historic G.T. support race for the 1982 British Grand Prix at Brands Hatch.

Tony Steele's Formula Junior 1.1-liter Lola at the start of the 1983 Barbon Manor Hill climb.

Bernard Horwood's 1.6-liter Lola 642-Auriga-Ford at Oulton Park for the Champion of Oulton car races.

Car no. 64, Meurig Roberts' 2-liter Lola-Ford T580, spins at Oulton Park during the 1984 F2000 Challenge.

John Foulston and John Brindley's 5.7-liter T530 finished fifth in the 1984 Donington Summer International unlimited sports car race.

Peter Milward, at the 1987 Historic G.T. Car Race, driving the rare Lola T70 5-liter Aston Martin-engined car that was once driven by John Surtees.

Patrick Tambay's Haas-Lola THL-2 with Ford-Cosworth TEC V-6 during the 1986 British Grand Prix at Brands Hatch.

Tambay's Haas-Lola THL-2/005 with Ford-Cosworth TEC V-6 finished in just three GPs during the 1986 season: Germany, Hungary, and Austria.

5.0-liter Lola T70-Aston Martin being driven by Peter Milward.

Larorousse team driver Philippe Alliot's LC88-Ford-Cosworth DFZ V-8, during the 1988 British Grand Prix at Silverstone.

I. Fidoe's 1.6-liter Ford-powered Lola 492 at the top bend of the Barbon Manor Hill Climb, 1989.

Damon Hill, in a 3-liter Ford-powered Lola T90/50, led the 1990 Silverstone F3000 race, until an electrical problem caused his retirement.

The Iconografix Photo Archive Series includes:

AMERICAN CULTURE

AUTOMOTIVE

TRACTORS AND CONSTRUCTION EQUIPMENT

RAILWAYS

TRUCKS

* This product is sold under license from Mack Trucks, Inc. All rights reserved.

The Iconografix Photo Album Series includes:

The Iconografix Photo Gallery Series includes:

All Iconografix books are available from direct mail specialty book dealers and bookstores worldwide, or can be ordered from the publisher. For book trade and distribution information or to add your name to our mailing list contact

Iconografix   Telephone: (715) 381-9755
PO Box 446   (800) 289-3504 (USA)
Hudson, Wisconsin, 54016   Fax: (715) 381-9756

MORE GREAT BOOKS FROM ICONOGRAFIX

VANDERBILT CUP RACE 1936 & 1937
Photo Archive ISBN 1-882256-66-2

FERRARI PININFARINA 1952-1996
Photo Archive ISBN 1-88225665-4

GT40 *Photo Archive*
ISBN 1-882256-64-6

McLAREN RACE CARS 1965-1996
Photo Album ISBN 1-882256-73-5

LEMANS 1950: THE BRIGGS CUNNINGHAM CAMPAIGN
Photo Archive ISBN 1-882256-21-2

CORVETTE PROTOTYPES & SHOW CARS *Photo Album*
ISBN 1-882256-77-8

SEBRING 12-HOUR RACE 1970
Photo Arhive ISBN 1-882256-20-4

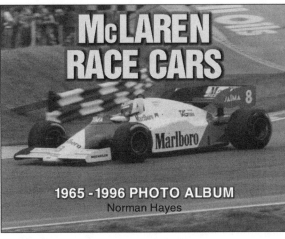

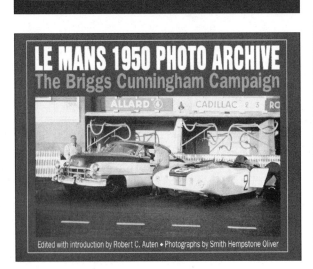

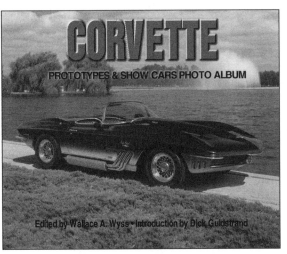